Georgia O'Keeffe

The Artist in the Desert

Prestel

Who is this lady?

She's wearing a black hat just like the cowboys
and ranchers do in the American West.

Her name was Georgia O'Keeffe,
and she was a famous painter.

In the background you can see the cliffs of
Ghost Ranch in the desert of New Mexico.
That's where Georgia O'Keeffe spent almost half her life.
She painted this landscape so often that nowadays
people call it O'Keeffe country.

Off to the Wild West!

When Georgia was a little girl, she lived with her family on a farm in Wisconsin. She used to love the adventure stories about Billy the Kid, Kit Carson, and the Wild West that her mother read to the children in the evenings.
That's when Georgia decided that Texas must be wonderful!

Years later, when she was a grown woman, Georgia still dreamt of Texas. She painted this watercolor when she was working in Texas as an art teacher.

The glowing colors express the excitement Georgia felt at the sight of the evening sky in the desert. She just painted what she saw on her walks: the endless prairie, up above it a fiery sunset, and the evening star that seems to shine so very brightly.

In this photograph Georgia stands next to Alfred Stieglitz. He was a famous photographer known all over the world. Alfred was so impressed by Georgia's drawings that he exhibited her work in his gallery in New York City.

Georgia and Alfred fell in love. Captivated by her beauty, over the years he took many photographs of her. After Georgia and Alfred married in 1924 they lived in a skyscraper, the Shelton Hotel, high up above the streets of New York City. They painted and photographed what they saw out of the windows of their apartment—by day and by night.

Can you see what's happening behind the illuminated windows?

In this picture Georgia painted the view looking down onto Lexington Avenue in New York City. The street at night always looked to her like "a very tall thin bottle with colored things going up and down inside it."

Summers in the country

The piece of drawing paper beside Georgia is still perfectly white.
Do you think she wants to paint the flowers you can see in front of her?

Alfred Stieglitz often photographed Georgia at Lake George.
For several years they spent the summer months there together.
In her garden by the lake, Georgia used to study every detail of
the plants: their forms, the lines, and all their different colors.
She was especially fascinated by the corn plant she painted in this
picture: its leaves, that grow up and down at the same time, and its
light-colored veins running down the center of the leaves like
flashes of lightning.

Gigantic flowers

What huge poppies! You can see right into them. They look so real you can almost smell their scent. Only they are much bigger than real poppies—as though you had zoomed in on them with a camera. It's hard to imagine how anyone could paint flowers like that!

Poppies, with their glowing red petals, were among Georgia's favorite flowers. She loved flowers, particularly because of their beautiful colors. When she lived in New York City, she started to make very large flower paintings. She wanted the people living in the city to see just how beautiful they were.

No one before Georgia had ever made such big paintings of flowers. Sometimes, her paintings take us up so close that it's hardly possible to recognize them as flowers anymore. When you look at these paintings it's like being a bee deep inside the head of a flower.

Georgia O'Keeffe painted many great flower pictures, which made her very famous.

lucky finds

The skull of an elk, brightly colored wild flowers, and red mountains in the desert —how strange!

The antlers in the clouds look so real, more like a photograph than a painting.

In the summer of 1929 Georgia and her friend Rebecca Strand visited the southwest of New Mexico for the first time. Georgia wanted to paint the desert landscape. But what should she paint? There were no flowers there!

On her walks through the desert she found stones and small pieces of wood, but she also found animal bones, bleached by the sun and the wind. She loved their beautiful shapes.

In this photograph you can see Georgia with one of her finds. Look how proud she is! She took the bones she found back to New York City where she painted pictures of the things that were so special to her in the desert.

After her first visit to New Mexico, she went back there every summer.

Colors of the desert

Georgia was fascinated by many things in nature,
by flowers and bones, and also by shells.
She used to collect them when she was
traveling and bring them back home with her.

The painting of the snail's shell is very large.
The shell is lying on red sand; in the background
there are bare, red hills. You can probably easily guess
where those hills are!

Georgia loved the red sandstone hills in New Mexico.
She once said: "All the earth colors of the painter's
palette are out there in the many miles of badlands.
The light Naples yellow through the ochers—orange
and red and purple earth—even the soft earth
greens."

This shell, washed clean, is not just white!
There are yellows and pinks there too: its delicate
colors gleam in the light of the evening sun.

So that's how you do it!

In this photograph Georgia is setting up her painting equipment in the desert.

With her new car she used to go exploring, far and wide. If she turned the driver's seat round, she even had enough room to work in her car. In that way she was protected from the noonday heat or from the evening cold.

At one of Georgia's favorite spots, the Black Place, you will find the grey hills you see in this painting. Whenever she saw them from a distance she was reminded of a herd of elephants: smooth, almost all the same size, with the same even furrows, and nearly white sand around their feet.

Blue mountain and red hills

In this painting the mountains of New Mexico seem
very close to us, too!

Once she went out exploring with her car. Traveling down
some difficult roads, Georgia discovered the Ghost Ranch region
and immediately fell in love with it. At first she used to go there
every summer to paint. In 1940 she bought the adobe house you
see in the photograph.

From her new house at Ghost Ranch she could see the desert
landscape with its red sandstone hills and, in the distance,
Pedernal, a flat-topped mountain of volcanic rock.

Georgia especially loved Pedernal, and gazed at it often
—watching the way the colors changed with the light.
She painted it again and again. Sometimes she used to say,
with a smile, that maybe if she painted it often enough
God would surely give it to her.

look, what's Georgia doing with that piece of Swiss cheese!

When she was a little girl she used to eat round the center of a jelly doughnut, saving the best for last. With the bones she collected she was also particularly fascinated with the holes where the animal's limbs used to be. She once said: "A pelvis bone has always been useful to any animal that has one—quite as useful as a head. I do not remember picking up the first one but I remember from when I first noticed them always knowing I would one day be painting them."

When Georgia held the white bones up against the sky in the sunshine one day, they looked very beautiful to her. It was as though she were looking through a telescope at the deep blue of the New Mexico sky—looking into infinity. And that's how she painted it.

21

A ladder to the moon

A long, homemade ladder used to lean against Georgia's house at
Ghost Ranch so that she could climb up onto the roof and gaze out at
the vast expanses of the desert landscape stretching out on all sides.
Sometimes she would even climb up there several times a day. At night
she could sleep there if she wanted, under the stars.

Why is there a ladder floating in the sky?

One evening Georgia was waiting for a friend. As she stood there,
leaning against the ladder, she gazed out into the wide, dark sky.
The night sky had a pale greenish-blue tinge. Far away the moon was
gleaming white. At that moment Georgia would have loved nothing
better than to fly to the moon. And then there was the ladder that she
had always wanted to put in a picture. She painted it floating above
the mountains, as though you could just climb up it to the moon.
In the picture everything is exactly as she wished it could have been
that evening.

Snow in the desert

When she saw a small adobe house in the village of Abiquiu, not far from Ghost Ranch, she had to have it! As well as a proper garden, it also had a patio with the long wall of the house and a door half way along it.

After Alfred Stieglitz passed away in 1946, Georgia moved from New York City to New Mexico for good. She often painted the wall of the inner courtyard with its black door—just the wall, the door, a few floor tiles, and the sky. In winter, too. Once even with snowflakes.

Apart from the times when her friends and her sisters came to stay, Georgia mostly lived quietly and alone in the desert. She enjoyed her life there, surrounded only by nature and the things she needed for her painting. She also had her dogs with her, two Chows which she referred to as "the people," and of which she was very proud.

Cooking with Georgia

Georgia was a keen cook. She loved fresh food and arranged it as elegantly and simply as the two poppies in her painting.

Would you like to try her vanilla ice cream? Here's the recipe:

Vanilla Ice Cream

2 egg yolks
1/2 cup honey
1 tsp. vanilla
2 pints whipping cream
Fresh fruit, as a topping

In a medium-sized bowl, mix the honey, egg yolks, and vanilla. Set them aside. Whip the 2 pints of cream in a large mixing bowl. Carefully fold the honey-and-egg-yolk mixture into the whipped cream. Set the ice cream mixture in the freezer for 30–45 minutes, or until it begins to freeze. Remove the bowl from the freezer and stir it gently until the mixture has an even texture. Spoon the ice cream into any preferred storage container and place it in the freezer to harden completely (about 2 hours). Serve the ice cream with fresh raspberries or other fresh fruit.

Georgia O'Keeffe's life

Georgia was born on November 15, 1887, on her family's farm in Wisconsin, near Sun Prairie, where she grew up with her six brothers and sisters. When she was twelve, and had her first drawing lessons, she already knew for sure that she "wanted to be an artist"!

After she left school she studied at various art schools and colleges. She became seriously ill in 1907. Soon after that her family was no longer able to pay for her to go on studying art—so for several years she worked as a commercial artist and as an art teacher.

In 1915 she was very impressed when her teacher talked of filling "a space in a beautiful way," and she started painting again. A friend of hers showed some of her drawings to the photographer and gallery-owner Alfred Stieglitz. In 1916 he exhibited Georgia's work for the first time at 291, his gallery in New York City. Georgia and Alfred fell in love and married in 1924. She then started to paint larger-than-life pictures of flowers. Many people greatly admired her work and she soon became famous.

In 1929 Georgia spent her first summer in the desert region of New Mexico. She returned there every summer after that while she spent the winter months in New York City with Alfred Stieglitz. In 1934, out exploring isolated areas with her car in New Mexico, she came upon the region of the Ghost Ranch. Georgia felt so at home in those surroundings that in 1940 she bought a house and a piece of land there. Later, in 1945, she bought a tumble-down ruin in Abiquiu, which she painstakingly renovated over the next three years.

Alfred Stieglitz died in 1946. Three years after his death Georgia moved to New Mexico, all on her own. In the desert she had everything she wanted. Photographers kept coming to photograph her there. By then she had long since become a famous painter. More and more museums presented her work at exhibitions. She was awarded numerous awards and a filmmaker even shot a documentary about her. Since she had no children of her own, she often helped the children in the village of Abiquiu and even payed the school fees for some of them. She still traveled to foreign countries until the age of 98.

Georgia died in Santa Fe in 1986. A year later the Georgia O'Keeffe Museum was opened. If you would like to visit the museum yourself one day, just go to: www.okeeffemuseum.org for more information.